To Ron's for Tea

A celebration of neurodiversity

Faith Truelove

AuthorHouse™
1663 Liberty Drive
Bloomington, IN 47403
www.authorhouse.com
Phone: 833-262-8899

Because of the dynamic nature of the Internet, any web addresses or links contained in this book may have changed since publication and may no longer be valid. The views expressed in this work are solely those of the author and do not necessarily reflect the views of the publisher, and the publisher hereby disclaims any responsibility for them.

This book is printed on acid-free paper.

ISBN: 978-1-7283-7611-0 (sc)
ISBN: 978-1-7283-7610-3 (e)

Print information available on the last page.

Published by AuthorHouse   11/03/2022

authorHOUSE®

Ron's view of life.

Ron was a very thoughtful boy,

Who was very difficult to annoy,

He permitted very odd behaviour,

In fact he often was the saviour,

He had learned to tolerate,

Many kids who do create,

Mayhem and chaos wherever they go,

Which can make most adults feel quite low,

He compared life to a magical tree,

Where those that grow there must be free.

To Ron's for Tea

When William Came for Tea

There was a boy; his name was Ron.

He was quite the perfect son.

He was often very caring,

Helping others who were wearing.

He had some friends who really tried

To conform, but their brains were wired

In a different way, not the "norm",

And they were unable to conform.

There was William Brown, who had ADHD.

Ron invited him to tea.

William was most delighted

To have been invited

To Ron's house because he desired

To have a friend who he admired.

William struggled to bond

With children of whom he was fond.

William tried to do his best,

But often he felt quite stressed.

He found it difficult to sit quietly.

And sadly, he infinitely

Jumped about all day at school
And disregarded every rule.
He drove the teachers to distraction.
They did not know what course of action
They could take make him calm.
It really caused them great alarm.
He found it difficult to learn.
He was, to his mum, a great concern.
The school had threatened to exclude him
Or keep him all day in the gym,
So he could just run around and shout,
"Will someone come and let me out?"
Ron could be very kind,
And he knew that other kids could find
Ways to make William's hackles rise
Because they knew he wasn't wise.
He wanted to be their friend,
But the wrong messages he would send.
So when Ron invited him to tea,
He was as excited as he could be.

Ron and William having tea.

He thought Ron's mum was really nice

And wanted to have a slice of her lovely cake,

That Ron told William she would make.

When William got to Ron's house he said,

"Where is the table and the chair?

I'd really like to sit down there.

I'll try to be still and quiet.

I'll do my best with all my might".

He had jam sandwiches and a sweet.

William could not stay on his seat.

He leapt about from settee to chair

As if he did not have a care.

He then jumped onto Ron's mum's bed

And broke the springs; Ron's mum saw red.

William had brought his small pet mouse

And let it loose in Ron's mum's house.

Ron's mum was not the delicate sort

But screamed, "That mouse, it must be caught.

I will not have it running free.

Keep it well away from me!"

Eventually, the mouse was caught.

Ron's mum was feeling rather fraught.

William said that he was sorry

To cause Ron's mum so much worry.

"I cannot help my ADHD,

You should not have given me jam for tea!"

Ron's mum said that William should

Get medication if he could.

It would improve his behaviour,

And it would be his saviour.

Ron's Mum, who was afraid of mice

keep it well
away from me
I hate mice!

When Billy Came for Tea

Billy Taylor was another boy in Ron's group.

Now, Billy only would eat soup.

He would not even eat ice cream;

It was so cold that it made him scream.

The soup was nice and warm he said.

He even ate it whilst in bed.

Ron also invited Billy for tea.

"My Mum has bought a piece of brie",

Said Ron, hoping that he could get Billy

To stop the soup fad that was silly.

It would not do his health much good

To eat soup instead of Yorkshire pud.

But alas, Billy failed to see

The point of just eating brie.

Ron's mum just made Billy soup

And added brie into the gloop.

Billy ate it willingly.

He couldn't even taste the brie.

Billy did not like too much noise

And played quietly with his toys.

He would not go into a crowded room,
Which really made his mother fume.
Billy could also get quite mad.
If his schedule changed, he felt quite bad.
He liked to know his day
Was predictable in every way.

Billy's soup bowl with brie added.

He found it difficult to cope

With even using different soap.

The soap he liked was in a bar,

Coloured yellow, and called coal tar.

If he ran right out of soap,

To make him wash, there was no hope!

He would not try another make,

Even if he was offered cake.

His mother had to often pop

Down the high street to shop

For soap that she could do without,

For Billy would just scream and shout,

"I want my yellow coal tar soap.

I feel I'm on a slippery slope!"

She'd enter every shop and enquire,

"Do you stock the soap that Bill desires?"

The answer was frequently a "No".

She did not know where else to go!

Poor Billy's mum was at her wit's end,

What she needed was a friend

That she could have a talk about

Billy's tendency to shout

If things did not go his way.

He always had a lot to say.

She was glad that he'd been asked for tea

For it may help him see

How other children could behave,

And how they didn't rant and rave.

Ron's mum could see straightaway

That there were fears she should allay.

Billy's brain was not the "norm",

And compared to others, did not conform.

He was autistic, it was plain to see.

To help him manage was the key.

That is not always bad,

Although it can make parents sad.

We all have different attributes,

Inherited from our DNA roots.

So make the most of what you've got.

Compared to some, you have a lot.

Be glad if you are not the "norm".

We should not all have to conform.

Billy trying to be quiet.

Don't shout!

tone it down!

no noise!

hush!

silence!

Be quiet!

When Sally Came for Tea

Another one of Ron's pals

Was a pretty girl called Sal.

She was great fun and loved to laugh.

She spent a long time in the bath.

Water was her favourite thing.

While in the bath, she loved to sing.

She splashed water everywhere,

On the floor and nearby chair.

Ron invited Sal to tea.

He also invited Sal's friend Bea.

Sal, she was a clumsy girl.

Her head was often in a whirl.

When tea was served, she knocked the plate.

Ron's mum came running in too late.

The plate tipped over on the floor.

Sal asked politely, "Do you have some more?"

"No, it has all been consumed".

Ron's Mum realised that a crisis loomed

For Sal was feeling very weak.

She needed food and would not be meek,

She asked Ron's mum if she could cook
Another recipe from Ron's mum's book.
Sal got out all the food she needed,
But Ron's mum's advice was not heeded.

sal singing in the bath.

She had told Sal to keep in mind

Not to use all the spices she could find.

Some were really very hot

And could cause your insides to rot.

Sal, she threw in everything

While she continued to loudly sing.

The dish was at last ready.

Sal tried to keep the tray quite steady.

Then oops! She tripped, not sure where.

The tray just went up in the air.

The food, it sprayed the walls and ceiling too.

Poor Sal, she did not know what to do.

She sat down upon the floor.

It looked as though there had been a war.

Potato, cheese, and gravy stuck to everything,

Even Ron's mum's wedding ring.

There were blobs of gravy everywhere;

Some were stuck in Ron's dad's hair.

Ron's mum laughed, and so did Bea.

It was the funniest thing to see.

Sal laughed until tears she shed.

She forgot that she had not been fed.

Ron's mum scraped the food from the wall.

She said, "Sal, this is all,

We have for you to eat just now".

Sal wanted to avoid a row,

So she ate the food somehow.

It was too hot with too much spice.

It really did not really taste too nice.

It almost blew Sal's head right off.

It gave her a terrific cough!

Sal knew that she'd put in too much spice,

And that was why it didn't taste too nice.

What a day it turned out to be,

And she'd only gone to Ron's for tea.

Ron's mum realised that what Sal had

Was dyspraxia, but it was not all bad.

Sal just needed a good chum

To help her out when she was glum.

Blobs of gravy and meat pie

When Edward Came for Tea

Ron had another friend who he

Often invited home for tea.

His name was Edward, and he had a stutter.

When he spoke, his heart would flutter.

He was a kind and thoughtful boy,

As well this, he could be coy.

He was often anxious and would utter

Words that really made him stutter.

When asked what he would like to eat,

Edward would say he'd, "I-I-I-I-ove some m-m-m-m-eat".

Ron had to listen for a while;

To get an answer was a trial.

But Edward was a kind and loving lad,

Because Ron liked him, he was glad.

He had a tough time generally,

So having good friends was the key.

Ron's mum cooked meat pie and peas.

It put Edward very much at ease.

He was looking forward to the lovely taste

Of pie and gravy made in haste.

Ron's mum didn't waste much time;

Her pie and gravy were sublime.
The dinner was table ready.
Ron's mum held the plates quite steady.
"L-L-Let me help you," kindly said Ed.
"I'm l-l-looking forward to being fed".
Edward delivered the plate carefully
To the table set for tea.
They all sat down to eat the food
Edward said that "It is very g-g-good".

Ron's Mum's meat pie

After tea, the boys were set on climbing trees.

They knew that they would scrape their knees.

They put jeans on, so they were protected.

But it would be harder than they expected.

Edward climbed to the top of the tree

And was excited by what he could see.

He saw a lovely bird of prey.

And then he decided to find a way

To get down to the ground again

Because it had begun to rain.

Edward found that he could not move at all.

He was so afraid that he would fall

From such a height he would surely die,

And never again eat meat pie.

He was terrified by his plight.

Dusk was falling, and it would soon be night.

He called to Ron to ask his dad

If he had a ladder, he would be glad.

So Ron ran to get some aid

For he could see the daylight fade.

It was a race to get him down by dark.

It was serious now and no lark.

Ron's dad quickly came to help.

Then he heard poor Edward yelp.

Edward had been in the tree

For what seemed an eternity.

Would he make it to the ground?

And would he end up safe and sound?

Ron's dad put the ladder against the tree

And clambered up to get Edward free.

They both climbed down; the ground was near,

The ground that he now felt was so dear.

He had never felt such mirth

As when his foot touched on the earth.

How glad he was; how good it felt.

He really thought his heart would melt.

"T-T-T-T-thank you, Ron's dad for saving me.

I-I-I-I'll never again climb to the top of a tree".

Ron's mum told Ron to be very patient with Ed

And to listen carefully to what he said.

Edward stuck up a tree

When Tommy Came for Tea

Tommy was a person who could cause Ron's day to worsen.

Tommy did not mean to cause trouble,

But he lived in his own small bubble.

He also did not have any filter.

He was often out of kilter.

He would just say what he thought,

Never mind the chaos it wrought.

Others could be quite upset,

But Tommy, he had no regret.

He did not understand the hurt

He caused others as he, "dished the dirt".

Tommy would say, "You have big ears".

Some kids just burst into tears.

Tommy may say, "You're too fat".

One kid hit him with a rounders bat.

It was quite plain to see

Why no one invited Tommy for tea.

Ron felt quite sorry for his plight.

He said, "Tom, you must come round tonight".

Tommy could not believe this was his chance

To have a friend who would enhance

His life as he was lonely now.

He needed to make friends, but how?

Tommy could not understand

Why he was often banned

From Scouts and boys' clubs in the town.

It always made him wear a frown.

He often said the wrong thing without thinking.

Then he'd feel his stomach sinking.

He needed to get his brain in gear

Before time passed another year.

Thank goodness that he'd been invited.

But was Ron being quite short-sighted?

Did he realise that Tommy may

Make Ron rue the very day that

He invited Tommy round to play?

Tommy said that he would try

To be his best but breathed a sigh.

It would be a gigantic task

To expect Tommy to do as he was asked.

Ron's Mum's ham and bread cut in triangles

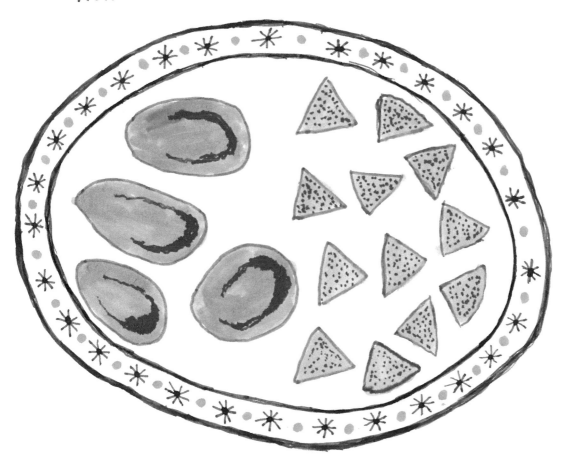

All went well initially.

Ron's mum asked what he would like for tea.

She had lovely scones and cakes and jam.

Then Tommy asked if she had ham.

"I do", she said, "but I need to save

Ham for the boys who do behave".

Tommy said, "I haven't messed up yet.

I haven't done anything I'd regret".

So Ron's mum gave him ham for tea

And bread in triangles that were crust-free.

It was all going very well until

He spied Ron's sister, who felt quite ill

When she realised that Tommy had his fill

Of food her mum had given him.

She kept away from him at school

For she knew that he'd broken every rule.

Suddenly, Tommy stood up and said,

"Why is your sister's face all red?

And why has she got ginger hair,

And green catlike eyes that stare?"

They all looked up and were aghast.

Ron's sister left the room so fast.

Ron's mum said, "Tommy, you must really think
Before you make other people's spirits sink".
Because Tommy hoped to be Ron's friend,
He did not want an early end
To his new-found relationship.
Maybe this was just a blip
That he must not repeat
If he wanted to eat
At Ron's house again.
Tommy did feel pain
For once he listened to what Ron's mum said,
And kept that thought within his head.
He really found it difficult to place
Himself in other people's space.
He decided that he would try
From now on just to breathe a sigh
Before he uttered any words
That would pierce a heart
Just like a sword.
Ron's mum thought Tommy displayed traits
Of ASD, and that was why he lacked mates.
But with help, he could be
A boy who would be invited round for tea.

Ron's sister with
staring green eyes

When Chance Came for Tea

Ron had a friend whose name was Chance.

She often just got up to dance.

There were things she did that worried him,

And often on just a whim.

She loved to be the main attraction.

She ensured this by her action.

Chance would do outrageous things,

Like hiding her mum's precious rings.

Her poor mother, she looked everywhere.

But Chance did not really care.

As long as she was having fun,

She did not care about what she had done.

Her actions could be quite bizarre.

She even played up in the car;

She would not put her seat belt on.

Her mother said, "You're not like Tom".

Her other child, he was so good.

He did everything he could

To help his mother manage Chance.

He always kept a similar stance.

Tom was a calm and thoughtful boy,

While Chance, she often would annoy

Everyone she met at school.

She often acted quite the fool.

The teachers were at their wits' end.

They did not know how it would end.

Chance shouted answers out in class.

She pushed a door and broke the glass.

The teacher thought her very rude

When she ate another child's food.

Ron invited her for tea

Because he thought it good to see

How very different she may be

In someone's house and not at school,

Where she could not act the fool.

Her mum dropped her off at four.

She was glad to see Chance's spirits soar.

Chance's heart leapt with glee

Because Ron had invited her to tea.

Chance had a friend who she thought cared.

She needed now to be prepared

To try and behave very well,

And not put Ron's mum through sheer hell.

chance and the broken glass

Ron asked, "Would you like to help me

Lay up the table now for tea?"

Chance said, "Ok, I will try to do

Anything that you ask me to.

I'd really like to please your mum.

I don't want her to think I'm dumb".

Ron was very pleased to hear

That he did not have much to fear.

The table was well laid up

Already now so they could sup.

It really was a lovely spread,

With cucumber sandwiches and fruit cake.

Chance must stay calm for Ron's sake.

She did not want to let him down

By trying to be a clown.

Suddenly, she had a strong desire

To just get up and poke the fire.

The cinders, they went everywhere.

Red sparks rose high into the air.

They quickly landed on the chair.

It smouldered for a minute or two.

Ron's mum tried to hit it with her shoe.

Ron got some water from the sink.

He doused the chair; he didn't think

That he could put the fire out.

Ron suddenly began to shout,

"Fire, fire! Phone the fire brigade

And ask for their immediate aid".

They promptly came and doused the flames.

"Who started this? What was their name?"

Everyone just stared Chance's way.

She wished she didn't have to stay

And listen to everyone chastise her.

Then they went away to confer.

Chance realised that she really had

Messed up this time, and she felt sad.

She really wanted to be Ron's friend,

But she didn't know how it would end.

She swore that she would never again

Cause others such a lot of pain.

Suddenly, she was full of fear.

She could have killed those she held most dear.

Chance realised she had to be more considerate
And think a bit and even wait
Before her actions tempted fate.
Also, before she did anything,
Could she hear alarm bells ring?
Ron's mum thought that Chance had ADHD,
And on the ASD spectrum she may also be.

Fireman putting out the fire.

When Rick Came for Tea

Ron had a friend called Rick

Who had a lot of different tics.

He would often shout rude things

And wave his arms about like wings.

He did things that were quite bizarre.

But he had ambitions to go far.

But the tics they made his life quite hard,

And he often felt his life was marred.

He moved his head in a strange way.

When he had a tic, he might say

Something people did not like

Whilst riding on his brother's bike.

Rick would sometimes shout,

"That man over there is quite stout!"

Ron liked him despite his tics

Because he ate Weetabix.

You may think this is very weird,

To like someone because they veered

Towards a certain breakfast cereal.

But to Ron, it had appeal.

In the Weetabix box

There were often things to entice
One to buy them as they were nice.
Like little soldiers and football cards,
Things that made kids think quite hard
Of which footballers to collect
To gain the set and to connect
With other kids who did the same,
Even if you didn't know their name.
They would become friends with you.
Even though they never knew
You at all before, they were pleased to have
A war with the soldiers collected from
Cereal packets in the shop,
This is where I must stop
And get back to explaining why
Ron asked Rick home for meat pie.
Ron found Rick an interesting fellow.
Personality wise, he was quite mellow.
Ron's mum liked Rick and said to Ron
That she would love to see his tics all gone.

Rick could not control his tics:
he just said what he thought.

He'd seen the main ed psych at school,

And she explained the general rule.

As he grew, the tics may just stay,

Or they may just fade away.

Rick really hoped the tics would go

And not return when he was low.

He was happy having tea with Ron

And ate the pie until it was gone.

He was concentrating solely

On the food; he was eating slowly.

When all his food had been consumed,

Rick's tics unfortunately resumed.

He was fine if he was concentrating

Or very seriously relating

A story that he wished to tell

About the time he unfortunately fell

In the road because he lost his footing.

Then he heard the cars all tooting.

Despite the tics and constant movement,

His friends could see some improvement

From how he was a year ago,

And they often told him so.

Rick had friends who loved him dear,

And they would often raise a cheer.

When they saw him in the street,

He was someone they were glad to meet.

Although Rick had an infirmity,

He was often invited round for tea.

Ron's mum, who was very wise,

Explained that she had surmised

That Rick had a syndrome called Tourette's,

But that she would wage a bet

That it would improve with time,

And his life would be sublime.

Rick's arms like wings.

When Rosie Came for Tea

Rosie was one of Ron's good mates.

But she was often in a state

For she struggled in every class.

She knew that she would never pass

An exam because she could not read too well,

And writing stories for her was hell.

It seemed that everyone could spell

And write good stories, except for her.

She thought that she would just ask Sir

To tell her of the reason why

She could barely scrape by.

She had trouble with English

For she could not distinguish

Between words that began with b and d,

She found it difficult to see

That they were not identical.

She would regularly fall

Into the trap of writing b's as d's

And she's as he's.

Ron was often there to aid

Poor Rosie as she tried to wade

Through reading books that she found hard.

She kept words written on a card

That she referred to when she could.

This really was not very good.

Which words should she use in her story

So that she could get some glory?

To cheer Rosie up, Ron said that he

Would love Rosie to come for tea.

He said, "Forget everything at school.

You are not the ultimate fool.

Just enjoy yourself for once,

And don't think of yourself as the class dunce".

At that moment, Rosie did feel low.

Her self-esteem was a source of woe.

Ron saw an opportunity to let her see

That she could finally be free

Of negative feelings that she had

For she often felt very bad

About the things she could not do.

This was sadly very true.

I tnew ot eht
sdoow esuaed
I evol koolign
ta eht seerts.
osla ti si os
lufecaep dna
neerg. ereht era
ynam sdirb nda
slamina ereht.

This is what Rosie saw when she was reading.

Ron's mum was very glad to see Rosie

And wanted to make her feel quite cosy.

She knew that she had found school tough

And had really had enough.

So Ron's mum really cheered her up.

She gave her fish and chips to sup.

Ron said it was her favourite meal

And would really make her feel

So much better than she did.

She was able to be totally rid

Of feelings about her poor ability

That threatened her mental stability.

Ron's mum said that Rosie must concentrate

On things that made her feel really great.

She asked Rosie how she was at sport.

And Rosie said that it made her fraught.

"What about painting and drawing?

Does that set your spirits soaring?"

"Yes it does", Rosie said. "I love to paint and draw.

It makes me want to do some more".

"Well, concentrate on that", said Ron's mum.

"It will stop you from feeling glum.

Don't dwell on things that you can't achieve.

Just concentrating on what you believe

Will help you feel proud and strong

As on life's path you go along".

Ron's mum said, "I think that you were born

With a condition that can make people scorn.

It's called dyslexia and can make words confusing.

And for you, it's not amusing.

So concentrate on things in which you can excel,

And for yourself, don't make life hell."

Fish chips and mushy peas.